D1053005

BLACK RAGE

MALCOLM X

Black Rage
MALCOLM X

A People in Focus Book

David R. Collins

 **DILLON PRESS**
New York

Maxwell Macmillan Canada
Toronto
Maxwell Macmillan International
New York   Oxford   Singapore   Sydney

Photo Credits

Cover and back image: AP/Wide World Photos
AP/Wide World Photos: 2, 51, 53, 54, 55, 56, 57, 58, 59, 61, 65, 68, 69, 70
UPI/Bettmann Newsphotos: 52, 60, 62, 63, 64, 66, 67

Library of Congress Cataloging-in-Publication Data

Collins, David R.
    Malcolm X : black rage / by David R. Collins.
        p.   cm. — (A People in focus book)
    Includes bibliographical references.
    Summary: A biography of the noted Black Muslim leader, looking back on
his life from the day of his assassination in 1965.
    ISBN 0-87518-498-7
    1. X, Malcolm, 1925-1965—Juvenile literature. 2. Black Muslims—Biography—
Juvenile literature. 3. Afro-Americans—Biography—Juvenile literature. [1. X,
Malcolm, 1925-1965. 2. Afro-Americans—Biography.] I. Title. II. Series.
BP223.Z8L5732 1992
320.5'4'092—dc20
[B]   91-39951

Dillon Press   Maxwell Macmillan Canada, Inc.
Macmillan Publishing Company   1200 Eglinton Avenue East
866 Third Avenue   Suite 200
New York, NY 10022   Don Mills, Ontario M3C 3N1

Macmillan Publishing Company is part of the Maxwell Communication Group
of Companies.

First edition

Printed in the United States of America

10 9 8 7 6 5 4 3 2 1

Contents

Introduction

He called himself the angriest black man in America, and when people heard him speak, they were convinced he was exactly that. Yet there were others who called him a man of peace, love, and hope. Whatever the case, Malcolm X, born Malcolm Little, lifted the voice of the frustrated black to a new volume. He demanded to be heard.

Alex Haley, the noted black writer who helped Malcolm X compile his autobiography—which he did not live to see published by Grove Press in 1965— seemed to understand Malcolm X well. "He held a mirror to the conscience of whites and blacks alike," said Haley, "and we did not like what we saw."

Just who was Malcolm X? How was it that he

managed in only 39 years to become one of the most influential people of the 20th century? In the pages that follow, you will come to know this man, his hopes, his dreams, and his anger. As disquieting as his voice was, it is a voice that should be remembered.

Chapter/One

Afternoon Nightmare

His hands clenching the steering wheel, the tall black man angled through the Sunday afternoon traffic of Harlem. A thin coating of sweat covered his body, lightly glazing his skin and seeping into his white shirt and dark suit. He was on his way to give another speech in front of another audience. Yet Malcolm X no longer welcomed each opportunity to share his views. Persistent threats on his life cast a gloomy shadow. They came through the mail, but more often they were voices on the telephone. Sometimes the calls were made to newspaper offices, while other times the death threats were recorded at police stations. Always the callers were unidentified, leaving Malcolm X angry and frustrated. Never a fan of the news media, he accused reporters of not taking the threats seriously. "They act like I'm jiving!" he told his supporters, but his protests went largely ignored. Despite his concerns, Malcolm refused to give up his speaking engagements. He needed to reach people. It was his mission.

People began arriving at Harlem's Audubon Ballroom shortly after one o'clock on the afternoon of February 21, 1965. It was a clear day, the weather pleasant enough to attract a good-size audience of eager followers. Not only was Malcolm X booked as a speaker, but the Reverend Milton Galamison was also scheduled to share the podium. Galamison was a militant minister from Brooklyn. Claiming "racial imbalance" in the public schools, he had spearheaded two one-day boycotts in New York City classrooms the year before. Unknown to the gathering as they assembled was that Galamison had begged out of this engagement, his calendar already crowded with activities. But it would not have mattered. When Malcolm X was scheduled to speak, he was the one people came to see and hear.

And the audience wanted to hear every word that Malcolm had to say. If ever there was a speaker who could fire up a crowd, Malcolm X was that speaker. The front rows were always packed with those who wanted to listen to every fiery word and capture every exciting gesture.

Men and women trickled in slowly, making their

way among the 400 wooden chairs that had been set up. There was no center aisle, but aisles were set up on either side.

People filing into the ballroom did not go through the usual search at the entrance. Because Malcolm thought the process made people feel uncomfortable, he ordered it stopped. And because of his recent unfavorable treatment in the press, reporters were also barred from this particular Sunday gathering. The ban went for both white and black newsmen, although one black UPI (United Press International) reporter was admitted after agreeing to remove his press badge.

Malcolm's sleek blue Oldsmobile cut through the midday traffic like a knife blade. He made good time, arriving at the Audubon Ballroom shortly before two o'clock. A quick glance at the stage revealed eight straight-backed brown chairs in a row behind the speaker's stand. A country scene painted on a canvas provided a calm, quiet background.

A small anteroom near the stage offered a meeting spot for Malcolm and his assistants. Brief greetings and remarks were exchanged, but the mood remained somber. Choosing a spot before a beat-up makeup mirror, Malcolm plopped down sideways on a chair and leaned heavily against the counter before him. He had decided that on this day he was not going to talk about himself. His own life had become so troubled, so jumbled. No, it was not going to be the topic for today.

But like it or not, that was one of the reasons people did come to hear Malcolm X. It was not just the message he carried, it was the messenger who carried it. For years, Malcolm X had been a source of dynamic black energy and pride—by fighting a battle against whites in heated oratory and defiant challenge. Gradually, that battle had spread into those of his own black race, as Malcolm X opposed individuals who would not accept his way, his thoughts, his manner of rebellion. No one ever accused Malcolm X of being meek and mild. He felt his convictions deeply, and he voiced them without hesitation or fear for his own well-being.

Yet the events the week before had clearly shaken Malcolm X. In the middle of the night his home had been firebombed. Molotov cocktails, tiny jars filled with gasoline and lighted short wicks, were hurled through the windows, exploding in flames. Frantic and frenzied, Malcolm and his wife, Betty, scooped up their children and ran out into the cold winter night. As tragic as the situation was, the entire event was viewed suspiciously by those who felt Malcolm X would do anything for publicity. Some believed him capable of and willing to burn down his own house to see his name in headlines.

Despite his denials, Malcolm X was still regarded with considerable doubt. Some who entered the

Audubon Ballroom that Sunday afternoon fully expected to hear the details of the recent firebombing. Others had been told their leader planned to announce a new program for liberating blacks.

Neither topic was in Malcolm's thoughts that afternoon. He was tired of talking about his own life, and the committee pledged to submit new proposals for black action had not completed its goals. Malcolm did not know what he was going to say, but he would find something to talk about. He always did. Yet on this particular day, the black leader felt unusually troubled. He had hoped for special speakers to be a part of the program. For one reason or another, they were not present. The ballroom was far from full. Would there be enough in donations to cover the rental expense? Sometimes the black leader wondered if the time would ever come when money would not be a worry.

But if Malcolm X was worried, the feeling was not contagious. At least it did not spread to one of his chief lieutenants, Brother Benjamin Goodman. Assigned to warm up the audience for Malcolm's entrance, Goodman lifted spirits and boosted enthusiasm. As usual, he laid out a general program of what was most needed by the black person in America. Then, Malcolm would follow with a detailed and forceful plan of how each step would be taken. That was the usual pattern.

People in the audience leaned forward as Goodman

concluded his remarks. Malcolm was coming. Malcolm was next. With his usual energy and enthusiasm, Brother Goodman warmed up the people. It was not that this speaker (Malcolm) merely had a message to share; it was that this speaker was willing to risk his life to do so.

Before Goodman was finished, applause began. People could not wait. Malcolm—they wanted Malcolm.

And there he was, the tall slender figure nodding approval to Brother Benjamin as he replaced him at the podium. The clapping grew louder, the smiles spreading throughout those assembled. As always, there were the words of friendship, of greeting.

"As-salaam alaikum. ("Peace be unto you.")

"Wa-alaikum salaam." ("And unto you be peace.")

Malcolm X smiled. He was among friends, among his people.

Without warning, there was a sudden disturbance in the audience. Two men jumped to their feet, bumping against their wooden chairs. There were angry shouts. Confused, people turned around to look at what was happening. From the sides of the stage, a couple of security men moved toward the commotion.

"Hold it! Hold it! Don't get so excited," Malcolm cautioned from the podium. He tried to calm the audience.

Then, from the front row, shots exploded. Caught totally off guard, Malcolm had no time to react. Bullets blasted into his chest, sending his body whirling back against the chairs behind him. Still the shots continued, shotgun blasts mingling with revolver explosions.

In the audience, screams and yells joined the roar of guns exploding. People leaped over chairs, some trying to reach the stage and others racing to escape. Malcolm's wife, Betty, after sheltering her own children from any assassin's bullets, scrambled forward toward her husband. "They're killing him!" she screamed. "They're killing my husband."

Confusion reigned in the ballroom. Once the firing stopped, people tried to determine what had happened. Someone ran in with a stretcher, hurriedly grabbed from a nearby hospital clinic. Malcolm's body was put on the canvas covering and whisked away, back to the same clinic.

Within minutes, the news raced through Harlem, the rest of New York City, and beyond. News broadcasters reported the shooting as soon as they got the first reports. But for a long time there was no official word regarding the condition of the black nationalist. Often the initial announcements were followed by a brief biography of the black militant leader. "Malcolm X was born Malcolm Little on May 19, 1925, in Omaha, Nebraska. . . ."

And as the newscasts continued, many people listened. Many people prayed.

Chapter/Two

Born into Trouble

Violence visited Malcolm X even before he was born—or before he was Malcolm X. His real name was Malcolm Little, the son of Rev. Earl and Louise Little. Not only was Reverend Little a Baptist minister, he was a devoted follower of Marcus Garvey. From his headquarters in New York City, Garvey had rallied thousands of backers across the nation who advocated the purity of the black race. Garvey felt that blacks would never achieve equality in white-dominated America, so he encouraged them to return to their native Africa, to run their own homeland. Garvey's suggestion raised as much controversy as support, and many white Americans viewed him and his backers with distrust, suspicion, even fear.

It was exactly such feelings that brought a band

of hooded Ku Klux Klan riders galloping to the Little home outside Omaha, Nebraska, late one night in March of 1925. When Louise Little appeared on the porch, the riders wanted to know where her husband was.

Being careful to show her pregnant condition to those surrounding the front porch, the woman answered. She told the men that her husband was preaching in Milwaukee.

Disgruntled and discouraged, the hooded intruders yelled threats. They told the woman to make her husband stop preaching about Marcus Garvey. The hooded men circled the house on their horses, breaking every windowpane with their gun butts. Another woman might have been left trembling, but Louise Little was used to such events. Her husband was always stirring up people, and when he wasn't causing problems for his family, he was a problem himself.

Earl Little was a man of rules. When a rule was broken, someone paid. Often it was his wife—or one of his eight children. Beatings were a way of life in the Little home. Earl found no problem with preaching the Lord's word and then returning home to administer the devil's discipline. From the moment he was born, Malcolm was punished least of the Little children. Why? He had inherited his mother's light skin coloring (her own father was white), a reddish brown shade, and hair of the same color. It set him off, made him look special.

Soon after Malcolm's birth, the family moved to Milwaukee. The stay was a brief one, the Littles next heading to a house on the outskirts of Lansing, Michigan. Little wanted to be able to raise food for his family if times became difficult. With the funds he earned preaching in area Baptist churches, Reverend Little hoped someday to own his own store. He openly shared his goal with his white neighbors.

The idea of a black store owner did not impress the folks in the Lansing area. Bootblacking and portering were respected occupations for blacks, but a black owning a store? Not only that, Earl Little chose to live outside the Lansing black district. Many area people thought he should be taught a lesson.

The lesson was taught with pistols and fire one night in 1929. This time the midnight intruders wore black hoods because they were members of the Black Legion. Malcolm was snatched from his bed by his mother and carried out in his underwear. Sadly the family watched their home burn to the ground, while white policemen and firemen stood around visiting with one another.

Mixed with those frightening memories were the exciting times when Earl Little carted young Malcolm to meetings of the Universal Negro Improvement

Association. As the boy stared at the handsome, shiny photos of the group's founder, Marcus Garvey, he heard talk of "Africa for Africans"—a time when blacks would run the entire continent across the ocean. When? No one could say for certain, but "it is coming," the minister would say. "One day, like a storm, it will be here."

But young boys do not live for the future. They live for the present. And it was a shrewd young Malcolm Little who learned the power of a small temper tantrum. Already aware that his lighter shade of skin was of value, he also learned the importance of a protest. When his brothers and sisters asked for buttered biscuits, their mother was quick to refuse. Even the quiet and sweet Wilfred was turned down when he asked.

But Malcolm would not be ignored. First he would ask, then he would demand a buttered biscuit.

At first, his mother refused. Then she ignored him. But Malcolm would not give up. The request turned to a yell, then a deafening cry. Finally, in desperation, Louise Little gave in. Malcolm got the buttered biscuit he wanted. He also learned that when he wanted something, he had to make some noise to get it. It was a lesson he never forgot.

At five, Malcolm started school. The Pleasant Grove School outside Lansing housed students in kindergarten through the eighth grade. The Little children were the only blacks in the area, but they were not mistreated. The white boys and girls called them "niggers" and "darkies," yet it was not meant to be cruel or vicious. Although blacks tolerated being called these names, they did not like it. There was simply nothing they could do about it.

A year later, tragedy struck the Little home. Ever since her husband had left the house one afternoon, Louise Little had had uneasy feelings. Something was wrong; she was sure of it. When Earl Little failed to return by nightfall, the woman became distraught. She hugged her children close, praying everything would be all right.

It was not to be.

Malcolm awoke to his mother's screams. Racing to the living room, he discovered two policemen trying to comfort her. They took her to the hospital, leaving a collection of worried children behind.

Word came early the next morning. Reverend Earl Little had been knocked on the head, then placed on the tracks for a streetcar to run over. For two and a half hours, the man had held on to life, his body almost cut in half. Then he died.

For a brief time, the Little house swarmed with visitors. But within weeks Louise Little found herself alone with a houseful of hungry mouths to feed. Insurance money was held back, the company claiming

Earl Little might have committed suicide. The thought was absurd! Who would kill himself by pounding his head in and sprawling over some streetcar tracks?

Louise found whatever jobs she could, mostly cleaning and sewing for white people in Lansing. Some people gossiped behind her back, snickering at how the insurance company had managed to ignore her claim. The older Little children dropped out of school, choosing to get jobs and take care of the younger kids at home.

The monthly bills easily outdistanced the money coming into the Little house. Since state officials provided regular welfare checks, they became constant visitors. Their questions annoyed Louise Little—she was sure they were trying to take away her children—and Malcolm often found his mother crying after a welfare worker's visit. Sometimes the officials questioned the children, too, asking them to come out onto the porch and talk about their mother.

Louise Little struggled to survive, to make a life for herself and her children. There were days when there wasn't a penny in the house. Dandelion greens were pulled and boiled as a meal, and the neighbors spread stories about the banquets of "fried grass" enjoyed by the Little family. When she learned of such gossip, Louise Little felt embarrassed and ashamed. For a proud woman, each day brought new misery. But she was determined to hold the family together.

The state welfare people seemed just as determined to split up the family. Malcolm resented the constant questions asked about his mother, his home, and his family. Why couldn't people just leave them alone? Certainly there were other poor people—the depression of the early 1930s had struck many families in and around Lansing as well as the rest of the country—but they didn't seem to be bothered all the time. The Littles were not the only area family on "relief." Yet Malcolm felt that a finger was being pointed at his family, and sometimes he could hear people talking about them and how poor they were. Every food item in the Little house seemed to be stamped "Not to Be Sold." The welfare distributors did not want recipients to peddle their groceries.

More and more often, Malcolm visited families in the area he knew who would give him a free meal. Shiny apples in Lansing stores often proved too tempting, and Malcolm would grab the appealing red fruit and make a quick getaway. He was not always quick enough, and his mother was ready with a whipping when necessary. But the pain of hunger soon won out over the fear of punishment, and once more Malcolm went looking for a free treat or two.

Time took its toll on Louise Little. So did the state welfare people. She reached out desperately for help. In 1935, a large, dark man from Lansing began spending time at the Little house. The children said nothing, but it was clear that the stranger made their mother laugh and enjoy life a bit. But then he stopped coming, and once more Louise Little slipped into a gloomy mood. She started talking to herself, drifting off into her own fantasy world where there was always plenty to eat and her family was secure.

The state welfare officials noticed the change in Louise Little. There was more and more talk about splitting up the family. Someone mentioned that the Gohannas family in the area was willing to take in Malcolm. They were older people, yet they had led the jumping and shouting whenever Rev. Earl Little preached. Malcolm liked the Gohannases.

With additional pressure put on her, Louise Little agreed to her son's move. Despite his desire to stay with the family, Malcolm realized the wisdom behind the change. Anyway, he could still visit his own family whenever he wanted.

The pressures on Louise Little became too great. In 1937, she suffered a complete mental breakdown. She was taken to the State Mental Hospital in Kalamazoo.

For 12-year-old Malcolm Little, the future looked dim. His father was dead, his mother in a mental hospital, his brothers and sisters scattered among whatever families would take them in. Often, the young boy's pillow was wet with tears—tears of confusion and anger.

Chapter / Three

Detention Center Kid

Malcolm watched his older brother's every move in the boxing ring at Lansing's Prudden Auditorium. Sweat glistened under the lights as Phil Little's muscles moved with precision timing. Tired sneakers slapped against the mat as limber feet danced in quick motion. It was late summer in 1937, Joe Louis had just punched his way to the heavyweight championship of the world, and every black boy in America hoped to follow Louis's example.

Of all the Little boys, Philbert showed the greatest promise as a boxer. More than one gym regular labeled the boy "a natural" and forecast his bright future in the ring. Malcolm, too, daydreamed of someday becoming a champion, yet his skinny frame showed small indication of developing any major muscular formations. He tried to box, largely to retain the admiration of his younger brother Reginald. Listing himself as the required 16 years rather than the 13 he was, Malcolm signed up for a bout. At 128 pounds, he qualified as a bantamweight.

Paired against a white boy named Bill Peterson, "Philbert Little's little brother" attracted a big crowd of family and friends. It was more than just a typical boxing match. Malcolm was representing his entire race. After all, the ring was the only place where a black could whip a white man and not get lynched for doing it.

Malcolm gave it his best shot. But he was no match for the tough, well-trained, and older Peterson. Time after time the black boy pulled himself from the canvas after being knocked down. By the time the final bell sounded, Malcolm was battered and beaten. His personal humiliation was even worse. How would he ever face his family and friends?

Of course, Malcolm was discouraged. But he was not a quitter. With fresh determination, he began a new struggle to become a boxer. He worked out at the gym each day, building his speed and timing on the smaller peanut bag. For power, he pounded the heavier bag, building the strength in his arms and shoulders. He jumped rope, did push-ups and pull-ups, often feeling that he would drown in his own sweat.

Finally Malcolm felt ready to fight Bill Peterson again. He signed up for the engagement. The fight was scheduled in Alma, Michigan, Peterson's hometown. At least, Malcolm thought, there wouldn't be as many of his neighborhood people at the fight. He was especially glad that his younger brother Reginald, who worshiped him, would not be in the audience. Not that Malcolm feared defeat. This time he felt ready, more confident. But anything could happen inside the ring.

With the sound of the opening bell of the match, Malcolm emerged from his corner, a beast ready to take on any opponent. Back and forth he danced, glad to stay out of Peterson's reach.

But ten seconds after the match began, it was all over. Peterson's glove connected with Malcolm's jaw, and then Malcolm's body connected with the hard canvas floor.

" . . . six-seven-eight-nine-ten!" The referee's voice rang out throughout the yelling crowd. Malcolm remained lying down, his back to the floor.

That fight ended the boy's short and undistinguished boxing career. Malcolm Little would never pose a threat to Joe Louis, or anyone else in the ring.

Neither did Malcolm choose to win special attention in the classroom, at least not for his conduct. Often, the warmth of his own bed kept him home, and when he did attend school, he won no honors for good behavior.

He enjoyed the role of school clown, firing back smart-aleck remarks to his teachers and depositing tacks on their chairs when they weren't looking. It was no major surprise, especially to Malcolm, when he was expelled.

It seemed clear to the authorities that living with the Gohannas family was not working for Malcolm. It was decided that he would be sent to a reform school.

But first he would spend time in a detention center. This one was located in Mason, Michigan, about 12 miles outside Lansing. The center was run by a Mrs. Swerlin and her husband. Malcolm didn't like the idea of living in a detention center, but at least, for the first time in his life, he would have a room all his own. As kind as the Swerlins were, they seemed always to be talking about "niggers," whether Malcolm was around or not. Upon returning to the center one day after visiting Lansing, Mr. Swerlin was filled with comments about the black section of town he had passed through. Malcolm stood nearby, within hearing range.

Mr. Swerlin wondered aloud how "niggers" could be happy when they were so poor.

Mrs. Swerlin just smiled and shook her head. It was just the way they were, she explained.

The Swerlins were not the only people who made such observations. Other white visitors, many of them local politicians, came to the center. They laughed and joked about "niggers" as if Malcolm was deaf to their remarks, some inhuman animal who had no feelings. Slowly, ever so slowly, an anger began to grow. What made white people superior? Were black people only a source of amusement, to be ridiculed?

Nonetheless, the Swerlins liked Malcolm. That was clear enough. They let him eat meals with them at their table. On weekends, they let him go into Lansing to hang out with other blacks. When it was time for Malcolm to head for the reform school, the Swerlins kept him on. They even enrolled him in Mason Junior High School, the only school in town. Nobody living at the detention home had ever attended the school before.

Malcolm soon won special attention at school. As the only black in his class, he quickly became known to students and teachers alike. He earned a spot on the basketball team and tried to ignore the sounds of people yelling "nigger" and "coon" whenever he appeared on the courts of opposing schools.

But it was impossible to ignore the comments of his own teachers. In history class, Mr. Williams loved telling "nigger jokes," each one of them poking fun at black people. The black person was always depicted as lazy and slow. Surely Mr. Williams had heard of the great black social reformer Frederick Douglass. And what of the noted black educators Booker T. Washington and George Washington Carver? Why couldn't Mr. Williams talk more about them?

Mr. Ostrowski, Malcolm's English teacher, was not quite as bad. But when the boy expressed a desire to become a lawyer someday, the teacher shot down such dreams. He told the boy he was reaching too high, that black boys just did not become lawyers. Now, maybe Malcolm could become a carpenter. He was good with his hands. Yes, that was within his reach—if the boy worked hard enough.

Malcolm was already working hard. He was earning the highest grades in the school. In his second semester in seventh grade, the students elected him president of his class. Malcolm was proud of what he'd accomplished. After all, he was only a kid from the detention center, and a black kid at that!

Many of Malcolm's older brothers and sisters had moved away from Lansing by this time and a visit from his half sister had a major effect on Malcolm. Ella had come from Boston to visit her relatives in Lansing. Never had Malcolm seen such a dark-skinned black. And Ella was so poised, so perfect. She took the family to visit Malcolm's mother, managing to get them all in at one time. Before she returned to Boston, she invited Malcolm to come and stay with her during the next summer vacation.

Malcolm could hardly wait!

Carrying a cardboard suitcase and wearing a green suit, Malcolm boarded a Greyhound bus and headed east to Boston in the summer of 1940. Ella was waiting at the depot and drove her visitor to her home in the Roxbury section of Boston. A new world was waiting.

Ella was a leader in Roxbury's "black society." She took Malcolm to meetings and parties, and he watched her socialize with charm and grace. People gathered together, displaying the latest in fashions and styles. They talked about world and national events, about business matters, about culture and entertainment. Their grammar was correct, their vocabulary impressive. These people were not arrogant. They were proud of who they were and what they were. It made Malcolm proud, too, just like when he scored a winning basket in a basketball game or earned a good report card. He felt happy about himself.

Roxbury on a Saturday night exploded with life. Blacks filled the streets, showing off their new cars and clothes. Others headed for an evening's fun at a favorite restaurant or nightclub. Smells of fried chicken and fish drifted on the air, mingling with the jukebox melodies of Duke Ellington and Erskine Hawkins. Malcolm spent hours walking the streets soaking in the atmosphere. Then he went home and told Ella everything he saw. She laughed, like some kind of fairy godmother, happy for everything he said and did.

And then the summer was over, all too soon, and the bus chugged back to Lansing. A different Malcolm Little rode the bus home. His mind bulged with wonderful memories of the summer. In Boston he had been a part of a mass of his own kind, blacks who lived well within their own community. In Lansing, he was one of a few blacks, different and separate. When a decision was made to place him with the Lyons family, a respected local black household, he showed no excitement. Even the fact that Malcolm would not have to go to reform school did not seem to lift his spirits.

Malcolm shrugged. It really didn't matter anymore to him. Lansing was Lansing. It wasn't Boston. He packed his things and went to live with the Lyons family. But his thoughts remained far away, and he dreamed of returning to Boston.

Soon his dream came true, two weeks after Malcolm finished the eighth grade. Somehow Ella managed to have custody of Malcolm transferred from Michigan to Massachusetts. He was going to live in Boston.

Malcolm, at last, was a happy person.

Chapter/Four

Downhill Slide

Malcolm gazed around the bus depot, looking for Ella. It was obvious that people were also staring at him. Small wonder. His light red hair was cut in a true hick style. It had none of the grease that city slickers usually applied. His head sat like a narrow Christmas tree ornament on his shoulders, which were covered in a green suit and topcoat, lending even more of a festive air. His ill-fitting pants revealed some three inches of white socks. His wrists and hands dangled out of his shirtsleeves, giving him a scarecrow look.

Ella threw her arms around her half brother, being careful not to reveal her amusement at his appearance. After all, he could learn how to dress later. The important thing was that he was with her, and Ella hoped she could help him.

Malcolm smiled. No mention was made of going back to the detention center. No one said anything about going back to school either. As far as getting a job went, he was told to look around and not be in any hurry.

Malcolm did exactly that. He roamed through the finer sections of Roxbury, his eyes taking in everything he saw. He talked to everyone he met and learned a great deal. Most of the blacks lived in a fantasy world. A janitor who worked in a bank claimed he was "in finance." A black woman who cleaned the dressing room in a theater considered herself "in the entertainment business." Errand boys for attorneys boasted they were "in law." If blacks did own their own homes, they often rented out rooms to help pay their bills. To Malcolm, members of his race were only fooling themselves, pretending to be something they weren't and pretending to have more than they really did.

Despite Ella's warnings, Malcolm headed to the ghetto part of town. The music blared louder, the lights blazed brighter, and people put on no false fronts. They were what they were, the tougher, rougher characters that populated Roxbury. Malcolm enjoyed their openness and the lack of pretense. He was drawn back to their world.

But Malcolm assumed a pretense of his own. He wanted people to think he was older than 14. He lowered his voice, strutted with a confident swagger.

He "conked" his hair, so it appeared straight and shiny.

And he made friends. Shorty at the pool hall had lived in Lansing, too, and the streetwise ball setter appointed himself a big brother to Malcolm. Shorty called Malcolm his "home boy" and promised to look out for him.

Hungry for friends, Malcolm tagged after Shorty. Soon he was shining shoes at the Roseland State Ballroom, enjoying the music and picking up cash from customers who were out for a good time. But it wasn't just slicking shoes that captured Malcolm's interest. Shorty showed him how to pick up extra money. Malcolm learned how to cater to everyone, whether they wanted drugs, booze, or women. He found out where card games were going on so the gamblers could spend their cash at them. In return for favors, Malcolm received big tips. He liked to carry his money in rolls that he could feel anytime he wanted.

Malcolm perfected his smile, his quick talk, and smooth manner. The tips increased. Soon the boy was placing his own bets, hoping to turn one dollar into five or ten. He took up smoking, too, and drinking.

One afternoon Malcolm walked in with a big surprise for Ella. He strutted across the living room floor, modeling a new blue zoot suit. The shoulders were padded and full. The wide-lapeled coat pinched his waist, then flared out. The pantlegs ballooned out a full 30 inches at the knee, narrowing to 12 inches at the ankle. Wing-tipped black shoes danced across the wooden surface of the floor, metal taps pecking out their own rhythm.

Ella flopped down on the sofa. What had happened to the boy she had brought from Michigan? Who was this stranger in her home? She did not know what to say.

But if Ella was speechless that day, she had much to say in the months that followed. She told him he was staying out too late. And she wanted to know where he was getting his money and with whom he was spending all his time. Ella's questions seldom received answers. When Malcolm *did* reply, he was curt and rude, his language strong and salty. He insisted he had to lead his own life.

The music at Roseland kept Malcolm dancing, and he tired of the shoeshining job. When he quit, Ella quickly found him a spot working at a drugstore only two blocks from home. She hoped he would meet some new friends, different from those he'd already come to know.

Laura Connors was certainly that. A high school girl with college dreams, she visited the drugstore often. She spent hours visiting with Malcolm as he made sodas at the counter. When Malcolm took her dancing at Roseland, Laura kept up with every step.

But despite Laura's obvious feelings toward Malcolm, he saw little more in her than a dance partner and friend. He wanted no commitments, no restraints. Ella encouraged the romance, and that didn't help the situation. Malcolm wanted to break the rules, not live within them. What money he earned went for new zoot suits, each one wilder and more daring. Malcolm lived for night life. He strutted along the streets at all hours. His buddies called him "Big Red" after he got his hair tinted scarlet.

And then came Sophia, a white girl looking for the fast life, too. She didn't dance like Laura. In fact, she lacked most of Laura's good qualities. But Sophia was white. A white girl on a black boy's arm got noticed. That was very important to Malcolm at this time.

The drugstore job got to be a drag. The boss expected Malcolm to be on time, even to respect customers. It was a lot to ask, too much. Nobody was going to tell him what to do. Malcolm quit the drugstore job and became a busboy at the Parker House. He carried the trays stacked with dirty plates and silverware from the dining room back to the kitchen's dishwashers.

And then, on the morning of December 7, 1941, the world exploded. Japanese planes staged a sneak attack on the United States naval base at Pearl Harbor. The lives of millions of Americans were changed. Malcolm Little's life was one of them.

Chapter/Five

The High Life

Across the country Americans entered the war effort. At 16, Malcolm was too young to sign up. But he was caught up in the feeling of change. He had stayed in Boston long enough. It was time for Malcolm to explore new sights.

"The Big Apple." That's what people called New York City. Even back in Michigan, Malcolm had heard stories about the exciting life in New York—Broadway, the Savoy Ballroom, Madison Square Garden. "Nothing like life in Harlem," some of the blacks had said. "You ain't lived until you been to the Apollo Theater, man. Music there is right out of heaven."

Ella voiced few objections about Malcolm's plans to head to New York City. At least, she thought, it would take him away from Sophia. But he had to have a job first. When a man from Ella's church mentioned that there were positions open on the railroad, Malcolm's hopes rose. The only catch was that employees had to be 21. That requirement posed no problem for Malcolm. When asked how old he was, Malcolm simply said he was 21. The fellow taking down information at the railway office did not even look up. Malcolm was hired.

Briefly, Malcolm worked as a dishwasher on the Boston to Washington, D.C., run. It was not a pleasurable experience. Often the train was loaded with white servicemen, many of them loud and annoying. Some wanted to know why he was not going to war. Like so many other blacks, Malcolm felt no guilt. It wasn't merely that he was too young. He also felt that since whites ran the country, they could fight to preserve it. He fought to keep his mouth shut, but often lost the fight and hurled back a smart-aleck reply. Malcolm was always glad when the train arrived in Washington.

When he could, Malcolm roamed around the nation's capital. Never had he seen blacks living in such filth as they did in some areas. Families crammed themselves into dirt-floor shacks, children half-clothed and begging. It seemed unbelievable that people could exist in such conditions, especially in the shadows of the nation's grandest and most glorious buildings. Couldn't the lawmakers see these sights?

Couldn't they hear the sounds of hunger and pain?

Soon Malcolm transferred from one railroad job to another. Now he became a food seller on the New Haven Line from Boston to New York City and back again. He could hardly wait to set foot in Harlem.

The event lived up to his expectations. He soon found a special spot at Small's Paradise, a popular Harlem nightclub. Never had the music sounded so sweet or the drinks tasted so smooth and pure. No one asked his age or background. Malcolm just fit in as if he'd always been there. During the day, black businessmen huddled around the circular bar, quietly drinking and talking. There was a certain class to the place, elegance even. At night, Small's came alive with a lively younger crowd, music shaking the place with rhythm and fun.

And from Small's, it was just a short taxicab trip over to the Apollo Theater, and to the Braddock Hotel, which attracted so many celebrities. Malcolm saw Billy Eckstine, Dinah Washington, Dizzy Gillespie, Billie Holiday, and so many more. This was the life!

This was the black man's territory. Few whites ventured into this land, reserved for those who came to dance in this African-American haven. Those who did fit in showed their admiration clearly with gawking eyes. That's the way it should be, Malcolm decided, whites looking up to blacks for a change.

Malcolm spent every free moment he could in
the Harlem arena. That's where he felt at home,
confident, important. He carried that attitude with him
back to the job. Customers on the railroad route
complained about his smart mouth, his cocky attitude.
Malcolm didn't care. If they didn't like his work, they
could fire him.

One day on the railroad run, a big, bulky white
soldier challenged Malcolm to a fight.

People turned toward Malcolm, wondering what
he would do. The boy nervously glanced around, faking
a smile. His stomach turned somersaults. Malcolm
agreed to fight if the challenger took off a few clothes.

The drunken man reeled. Quickly he slipped out
of his overcoat. Off came his uniform jacket. A few
soldiers in the railroad car started laughing. When the
soldier next slipped off his shirt and undershirt, the
entire group hooted and howled. Malcolm smirked in
triumph, then retreated out the door. He felt like a
champion, beating the white man by using his mind.
It felt good, mighty good.

Malcolm earned a reputation for a smart mouth,
always having the last word. Co-workers who tried to
calm his loud and wild outbursts met no success.
Malcolm was like a proud, strutting rooster. Most of the
time he was half drunk on liquor or half high on reefer
(marijuana cigarettes). With his flaming red hair, his

bright zoot suits, and his orange knob-toed shoes, he could have joined any circus as a clown. But in his own eyes, Malcolm was cool.

But the New Haven Line officials failed to find Malcolm as cool as he thought he was. Complaints rolled in, one bumping into the other. His firing came as no surprise.

Malcolm spent his last paycheck on a trip back to Michigan. Lansing was not prepared for the changed visitor. With his super conked hair and wild suits, he appeared like some creature from outer space. His speech was just as alarming. "Skin me, Daddy-O!" he'd greet old friends, his hand outstretched. "How's the man movin' and groovin'?" Mrs. Swerlin could only shake her head in disbelief. A visit to see his mother at the state hospital in Kalamazoo shook Malcolm. She barely recognized him, and they had very little to say to one another.

Broke when he returned to New York City, Malcolm had to find a job quickly. All he really knew was railroad work, so he managed to get work through a different railroad, the Seaboard Line. The job didn't last. Word got back to Seaboard officials of Malcolm's past on the New Haven Line. That ended that—fast.

Having made friends with many people at Small's Paradise, Malcolm landed a job there as a waiter. The rules were simple: no lateness, no stealing, no laziness, no smart mouthing, no hustling the customers. Malcolm agreed.

Malcolm took to his new job eagerly, and the customers took to him, too. He had already made many friends just hanging around Small's. They liked him, and he dripped with sweetness. He quickly sized up each customer, deciding what kind of act each would appreciate. Malcolm knew the right words, the right tone, could mean a bigger tip, and he was all for that.

On land and at sea, World War II raged on. But Malcolm Little was touched only by what he heard on the radio and read in newspaper headlines. Small's Paradise remained a sheltered world, offering hours of pleasure for fun seekers. Many were hardworking New Yorkers, out for a night on the town. But there were plenty of Harlem's seedier characters—dope peddlers, thieves, pimps, professional gamblers. They all told their own stories, liquor loosening their tongues, and 17-year-old Malcolm Little listened closely. He pumped his salary and tips back into the betting world, hoping and dreaming of the day when he would hit it big.

Not only did Malcolm work with these people at Small's, he lived with them, too. He found sleeping rooms in different spots, always trying to save on money so he would have more to bet. Often he welcomed Sophia from Boston, introducing her to his Harlem friends and hangouts. She came, even after

she had married a serviceman. It didn't matter to
her, and it certainly didn't matter to Malcolm. It was
even more exciting.

But when Malcolm hustled a customer at Small's,
there was no undoing it. Not only was he fired, he was
barred from the premises. When his friend Sammy
suggested selling drugs, Malcolm jumped at the chance.

With all his friends, Malcolm proved an able
salesman. He was sly and slick, and he knew a lot of
musicians in the Harlem nightclub neighborhood who
enjoyed smoking reefer. He got his marijuana from
merchant seamen and had no trouble unloading it. But
he also knew that there was more money to be made
handling cocaine and heroin. Malcolm wanted the
most money out of the time he put in. Some of his
dealer friends told of earning $100 a day and more
peddling coke or "H." But for the time being, selling
reefer kept a roll of money in his pockets. Often it was
$50 or $60, a fortune for a 17-year-old black.

When he wasn't on the street selling drugs, Malcolm
relaxed in a movie theater, soaking up a Humphrey
Bogart or Jimmy Cagney flick. He liked the tough guy
films, filled with action, bad guys outwitting the good
guys. Malcolm himself began carrying a "gat," a little
.25 automatic. It slipped neatly under his belt down the
center of his back. Cops never patted there when they
searched anyone.

And Malcolm did, indeed, get searched. It didn't take the Harlem narcotics squad long to know when a new drug peddler was on the streets. They watched Malcolm closely, and he knew he was being watched. Whenever he was stopped and searched, he loudly warned officials he didn't want them planting any drugs or a weapon on him. Usually he made sure there were other blacks around. If officials would try to claim he was carrying drugs or armed, he could declare he was being set up. He knew the cops wouldn't risk a big racial outbreak.

Malcolm took to riding the rails again. He still had some employee identification cards that most conductors didn't inspect closely, and he happily jumped on one train after another. Always there was a band on the road, too, with musicians looking for drugs. Malcolm catered to their needs, always staying a step ahead of the law.

By 1943, Malcolm was not only dodging law enforcement officials but the United States draft system, too. He wanted no part of the military service. That was no way to make money, and there were too many rules to follow. Malcolm liked doing what he wanted with no one giving him orders. When the authorities finally pulled him in for a checkup, Malcolm put on a star performance. Dressed in his wildest zoot suit, he slipped into his yellow, knob-toed shoes and frizzled his hair into a reddish bush. Then he strutted in to meet the doctor. For the next half hour Malcolm raved about wanting to go down South and organize other blacks. Yes, that would be great! Then they could take over. The doctor shook his head at the wild ravings and declared Malcolm ineligible for the draft.

Malcolm discovered there was big money to be made in blackjack and poker games. He'd always liked cards and knew how to sniff out where a big game was going on in Harlem. As much as $500 graced the table. The locker room at Grand Central Station was a favorite gathering spot for the black railroad men. Malcolm became a regular player.

One night Malcolm spotted a blackjack dealer shooting cards off the bottom of the deck. Malcolm pulled his gun out and pointed it in the dealer's face. Quickly the dealer straightened up his act and stopped cheating.

But the police around Grand Central Station put the pressure on Malcolm to clean up his own act. He was told to stay away from the railroad terminal unless he had a ticket to ride somewhere.

Knowing the railroad officials were watching out for him, and the narcotics squad was keeping an eye on him, too, Malcolm felt new pressures. He decided to slow down on the drug selling. Maybe he should peddle enough to keep himself well supplied, but not take any unnecessary risks of getting caught. But he needed to find something else to keep money in his pockets. Lacking education and work experience, his choices were few. He wasn't about to find some nothing job that paid little but required a lot. He'd seen too many other ways of making money easily. Everywhere he turned, he saw guys running numbers games, betting every penny they had in hopes of striking it rich. Malcolm had already tasted that profession. There were the sex merchants, too, men offering women for a few hours or a night of fun. There was big money in that. Burglars bragged of how easy it was to break into homes and businesses. Stickup artists talked big, too, sharing their stories of holding up stores or unsuspecting people on the street.

Malcolm picked the latter route. He added to his "hardware," choosing a .38 or sometimes a .45 to carry on a heist. The .25 he already owned just didn't look threatening enough. A little cocaine before each job provided him with some extra courage. He headed out of town to pull his robberies and stickups, not wanting to risk being recognized. No big jobs such as banks. Corner liquor stores or drugstores offered quick cash in a manner of minutes.

But Malcolm soon tired of working alone. There was a lot of money just waiting to be swiped around Boston. He knew Sammy would be game for making some fast cash. Then there was his friend Rudy. And with Sophia, there were chances to really expand the entire operation. Maybe pull her sister in, too. Sophia and her sister could go door to door, pretending to sell something. This could get them inside people's homes. Once inside, the girls could look the places over, searching for anything valuable inside. Then they could report what they'd found, letting Malcolm, Sammy, and Rudy come back to rob the homes later. Malcolm soon had the entire plan in operation.

It worked. Time after time, it worked. There were a few close calls, but Malcolm didn't worry. The drugs helped. They blurred his mind, scared away the fear of being caught.

Then it happened. Malcolm left a stolen watch at a jewelry store to be repaired. Two days later he went to pick it up. What he didn't know was that all the jewelers in Boston had been alerted about the lost watch. The jewelry store was carefully staked out by detectives. The minute Malcolm reached for the watch, a detective reached for him and ordered him into the back room.

Just then, another black man walked into the store. The detective thought he was with Malcolm. Remembering the gun he was carrying, Malcolm thought a split second about shooting. Something held him back. He even told the detective to take his gun.

It was a wise decision. Later, Malcolm learned the

detective was not alone. His partner was watching everything.

The others in the burglary ring were rounded up; the stolen goods that had not been sold were recovered. It was a saddened Malcolm Little who stood before a Middlesex County court judge for sentencing in February of 1946. He was 20 years old.

"You are hereby sentenced to serve a term of ten years in the Charlestown State Prison," the judge declared.

Ten years. Malcolm Little, his head hanging low on his chest, trudged slowly from the courtroom.

Harlem in the 1940s

The nightlife in Harlem appealed to many young blacks.

Elijah Muhammad changed Malcolm's life.

*More and more churches asked the
young preacher to speak to their congregations.*

*Martin Luther King, Jr. and Malcolm X,
united briefly by a handshake*

A huge crowd listens to Malcolm at a rally in Harlem.

Malcolm had a tense relationship with the press, which he often accused of twisting his words.

As Malcolm looks on, Elijah Muhammad preaches
separation instead of integration.

Mecca was the final and most
important stop on Malcolm's trip to the Middle East.

Malcolm prays with Muslim leaders in Cairo, Egypt.

Malcolm arrives home after his tour of the Middle East.

Malcolm announces the formation of his new Muslim sect.

Malcolm holds his daughter Ilysah.

Malcolm arrives home after a firebomb was tossed into his house, severely damaging it.

Malcolm's body is carried from the Audubon Ballroom.

Bullet holes where Malcolm X was shot

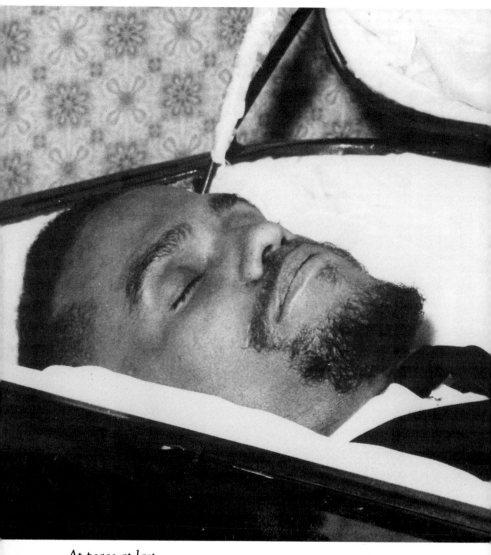

At peace at last

Betty X at the graveside

Mourners grieve the death of Malcolm X.

Chapter/Six

Behind Bars

The sound of the prison door slamming shut echoed through Malcolm's ears. Ten years. No longer was he a person, a name; now he was merely a number. He heard it called out, saw it stenciled on every item of his clothing.

Charlestown Prison was a human cage that had been built in 1805. Each cell lacked running water, and Malcolm found he could lie on his cot and touch both walls. A covered pail in the corner served as a toilet.

From the moment he entered Charlestown, Malcolm showed no interest in becoming an ideal inmate. Both the prison psychologist and the chaplain got an ample dose of the new inmate's gutter language. He wanted no part of them and he told them so. Nor did he have any use for the prison guards and other inmates—unless they could help him out. Malcolm soon learned that drugs were available at the right price. A kind and faithful Ella paid regular visits and sent him money. The cash slipped through his fingers swiftly, right into the hands of those who would supply him with anything that could get him high.

High or not, Malcolm spent much of his time in solitary confinement. He was sent there as punishment for tossing things out of his cell, hurling his cafeteria tray to the floor, refusing to answer his number at roll call—anything to cause problems, to disrupt the system.

When Malcolm wasn't yelling at prison officials, he was yelling at God. It was God's fault the earth was such a miserable place. It was God's fault people did wrong things and hated one another. It was God's fault for every bad thing in the world. And as far as the Bible was concerned, he wanted none of that, either. Not only would he reject anyone approaching him about the Bible, he used the strongest language he knew to describe what was in it.

Malcolm's irreverent attitude earned him the nickname "Satan." Even the toughest men in his cellblock shied away from him. Only a fellow named Bimbi seemed to like him, but then again Bimbi liked everyone. Inmates and guards surrounded the man, eager to hear what he had to say. And Bimbi had plenty to say. He knew much about so many topics—history, music, human behavior. Bimbi talked about religion, too. He didn't try to convert anyone to a particular faith. He merely explained how people worshiped and why. It was all so sensible, the way Bimbi spoke, so clear and reasonable. Malcolm's outbursts ceased. With Bimbi's encouragement, he began using the prison library more. He enrolled in a correspondence course to build his writing skills.

In about a year Malcolm was transferred to the prison at Concord. It was a more modern institution, cleaner and quieter.

So was Malcolm. He was reading and writing more, using a mind that had been idly resting. His brother Philbert wrote him often, telling him about "the natural religion for the black man." It was founded and based on the nation of Islam, and Allah was the supreme power. Philbert encouraged Malcolm to pray to Allah for deliverance.

His brother Reginald wrote him, too, lending more help and support. Reginald encouraged Malcolm to give up eating pork and smoking cigarettes. He promised to help him get out of prison.

By this time, that's all Malcolm could think about—getting out of prison. He hated being kept like some animal. Giving up pork and cigarettes was a small price to pay if it helped get out of prison faster, he believed.

More letters poured in from his family. Some

days he would receive four or five. His brothers and sisters had not given up on Malcolm. They all urged him to accept the teachings of the Honorable Elijah Muhammad.

Certainly, Ella had not given up. In 1948, she managed to get her half brother transferred to the Norfolk, Massachusetts, prison colony. This new facility had flush toilets, walls rather than bars, and clean, fresh air with regular exercise periods for the inmates. Prisoners earned privileges and were treated with respect. Malcolm felt like he was in a new world.

The library at the Norfolk prison boasted countless volumes about history and religion. Inmates were free to wander the aisles, picking out books of their choice. Malcolm could not get enough of this world. He read like he had never read before, searching for knowledge, reaching for answers to questions about life. Gone was the rebellious Malcolm Little who had first entered through prison doors. Now he sensed a purpose for his time, a wish to make the future meaningful.

Letters and visits from family members added further support. His brothers and sisters all seemed so comforted and satisfied with their new faith. Converted to the natural religion for the black man, they shared their thoughts with Malcolm. His brother Reginald became the family spokesman for this new and glorious Muslim faith. He spoke of the great and kind wisdom of Allah, a man and god who knew everything. He also spoke of the devil, a man working on behalf of evil in the world.

"What do you mean?" Malcolm wondered, his mind whirling. How could anyone know this devil, this evil spirit? Where was this devil? Who was this devil?

Reginald pointed at the white inmates nearby and their visitors. "Them," he said. "The white man is the devil."

A confused Malcolm thought about what his brother had said. It was white people who had killed his father, then swindled his mother out of insurance money and led her to the asylum in Kalamazoo. There were the white kids at school, teachers, too, always calling them "niggers." Maybe it wasn't just a label. It was meant to be cruel. And there was Mr. Ostrowski, who suggested Malcolm pursue carpentry when he'd expressed an interest in law. What good was he?

Images of other white people passed through his mind. Social workers who pretended to be friends but really weren't. There were the arrogant whites who stopped for a shoeshine and shared their latest black jokes, then failed to even tip a nickel. There were the loud white servicemen on the trains from Boston to New York, and crude and rude customers at the Parker House, where he briefly bussed tables. How about that white jeweler who helped him get caught? Yes, there was a lot of sense to what Reginald said. White people were bad and wanted to use the blacks. All those history books Malcolm had read told the real story. The whites had brought the blacks over as slaves for them to do the white man's work. Therefore, the white man wouldn't get his own hands black. But blacks being equal? What a joke!

Weeks slipped into months, months into years. As time passed, Malcolm listened to Reginald more closely. For hours Reginald talked about "the devil white man" and "the brainwashed black man." Malcolm heard his brother talk about how the white man's world was on the way down. It was on the way out.

How had the change occurred? Malcolm had many questions. Who had brought the changes?

Reginald had the answers. He told Malcolm that God was a man named Allah. Allah had 360 degrees of knowledge, according to Reginald. That represented all knowledge. Allah knew everything. His religion was called Islam and those who believed were Muslims. Allah's messenger on earth was a man named Elijah Muhammad, a black man like them. He had been born on a farm in Georgia.

Allah had given Elijah Muhammad special powers to carry out his duties. The blacks were the chosen people of the Islam faith. If they followed the religion as Muslims, blacks would find new happiness.

Slowly and steadily, Malcolm became a Muslim, a follower of the Islam religion. All he heard and read about the faith seemed to make sense. Christianity was the white man's way of keeping black people in line. It was a faith built on power, power for the white man. It was the Islam faith that offered hope to the black man. Reginald convinced Malcolm that Allah was waiting to help him if Malcolm would accept Allah as his god.

Finally, Malcolm made a big decision. He wrote a letter to Elijah Muhammad. Malcolm wrote what his family had been telling him about the Muslim faith. Despite his own awareness that his spelling and grammar were bad, Malcolm felt good about the letter. He sent it to Elijah, who was living in Chicago.

Weeks passed. Then an answer came. Elijah Muhammad welcomed Malcolm as a Muslim, a follower of Allah. Though Malcolm was a prison inmate, Elijah made little of it. He claimed that white men forced blacks into lives of crime by oppressing them and forcing them into poor jobs. Inside the letter was a five-dollar bill.

Malcolm was thrilled. He pledged that he would write every day to Elijah Muhammad. He also promised that he would write a letter a day to one of his brothers or sisters who had led him toward this moment. Malcolm wanted nothing to do with the prison world. At Norfolk, he became a hermit. All he wanted to do was to think about his newfound Muslim faith, to read about it, and to write to those who shared it. Proudly he wrote on his cell wall: I AM SAVED.

Malcolm read everything about black history he could find. It became clear, just as Elijah had said, that slavery was the white man's worst crime. No matter what the white man would do, nothing could erase the blood on his hands from that evil time in history. The black man had always been the white man's slave—and still was. Only a devoted effort could change the black man's role, with the help of Allah, that is.

With his constant reading and understanding, Malcolm also began sharing. He talked about Elijah and his teachings, the black man's plight in history, the possibility of a brighter future. Soon he began speaking to small groups of his fellow black inmates, to anyone who would listen.

There was a debating group at Norfolk prison colony to which Malcolm was attracted. He enjoyed researching a topic, taking one side of an issue, and arguing against opponents. It was a challenge of the mind, stimulating, creative. Malcolm loved debating. Should military training be compulsory? Did William Shakespeare really write all those plays himself? Research was fun!

Without warning, Malcolm faced a major dilemma. His brother Reginald visited him, voicing criticisms of

Elijah Muhammad. The problem boiled down to Reginald breaking a major rule of the Muslim faith. He had carried on a relationship with one of the Muslim temple secretaries. When Elijah Muhammad found out, he had suspended Reginald from the faith. It was a bitter and angry Reginald who spoke out.

Malcolm was torn between his faith and his brother. He wrote to Elijah Muhammad, seeking some sense of direction. The answer from the messenger of Allah was quick and clear. Elijah told Malcolm that if he challenged Allah and the truth, it was a sign of Malcolm's own personal weakness. No person, even a brother, was worth challenging the wisdom and faith in Allah.

Malcolm chose his faith over his brother. Never again would Reginald totally enjoy his brother's love and respect. Malcolm was a devoted Muslim. He would follow Allah and the Islam faith. Elijah Muhammad had won out.

Malcolm's outspoken manner caused many prison officials to wonder about him. Even some of his fellow black inmates questioned his total dedication to the Muslim faith. Plans were put in motion to get him transferred to another prison. Early in 1951, Malcolm was moved back to Charlestown Prison. He had read so many books that he now wore his first pair of eyeglasses. He was totally caught up in the Islam faith.

While attending a Bible class, he could not resist putting a white instructor on the spot. Malcolm threw questions at the teacher, asking him about the color of Jesus' disciple Paul—and even the color of Jesus himself! The instructor was clearly surprised and grasped for answers. He declared Jesus was brown.

Malcolm let the answer slide by. It was a reasonable compromise. But within hours, the prison buzzed with stories of the Bible class encounter. Once again, Malcolm had made his presence known. He liked the feeling of being noticed. Never had he been one to shy away from attention.

In August of 1952, Malcolm Little was paroled from prison. He had served seven years of a ten-year sentence. "Freedom." How great that word sounded! One thing was certain—Malcolm had a sense of direction. The Islamic religion had wrapped itself firmly into his thinking. Perhaps he could put the past behind him. He was eager to turn a new page in his life, and Elijah Muhammad was sure to play an important part in it.

Chapter / Seven

All for Allah

Happily Malcolm walked through the doors of the Turkish bath. The first thing he wanted to do with his new freedom was to steam all the physical taint of prison out of his body. Once that job was done, he headed to Ella's place for a good night's rest.

Ella had no interest in the Islam faith and the Muslims. She was happy enough that her brother and other family members appeared content with their new faith, but she did not share their feelings about Allah, Elijah Muhammad, and the rest of it. She simply wanted peace in the family, and a better life for Malcolm.

In an effort to start fresh, Malcolm headed west to Detroit. He had relatives there. His brother Wilfred managed a furniture store and offered Malcolm a job as a salesman. Quickly he accepted.

But Malcolm's thoughts were clearly on more important matters than selling sofas and chairs. Detroit boasted a heavy black population, many of whom were still not aware of Allah's teachings. Malcolm was not the only person who knew that. From his home base in Chicago, Elijah Muhammad knew it, too. Eager to carry Allah's teachings across the country, Elijah Muhammad was always on the lookout for new lieutenants in his organization. Certainly Malcolm looked like a likely prospect. Hadn't he held to the faith rather than side with his brother Reginald? Certainly Malcolm's letters from prison reflected his ever-increasing devotion to the faith. Yes, Elijah had his eye on Malcolm.

As for Malcolm himself, his feelings of love for the Muslim faith and Elijah as a messenger of Allah grew stronger every day. Living with Wilfred in Detroit, Malcolm saw how the Muslim faith carried itself into the family unit. Wilfred's family practiced the faith closely, from the moment they got up in the morning until they retired at night. Wilfred arose first, preparing his way for the others in the household. After all, he was the family provider and protector. He set the example. There followed the washing of the right hand, then the left. The teeth were brushed thoroughly and rinsed three times. The nostrils were also carefully cleansed. A shower completed this morning purification process, and then the family met for prayer.

First, the members of the family wished each other a wish of peace. Then the family knelt onto the spread prayer rug, facing the sun, near the horizon. They were joining some 725 million other Muslims in facing the East, praying toward the holy city of Mecca.

They recited, in Arabic, the family prayer, in unity and reverence. "I perform the morning prayer to Allah, the Most High, Allah is the greatest. Glory to Thee O Allah, Thine is the praise, Blessed is Thy Name, and Exalted is Thy Majesty. I bear witness that nothing deserves to be served or worshiped besides Thee."

Then the family members went out into the world, to school or jobs, carrying the gentle and loving spirit reflected by the prayers that began each day. Malcolm welcomed each morning. It was far removed from the ugliness of prison life.

On Wednesdays, Fridays, and Sundays, the Muslim faithful in Detroit gathered in Temple One to share togetherness and prayer. There was a feeling of community and strength among those attending.

But for Malcolm, there was also a feeling that not enough black people understood the greatness of Allah, the joy of his teachings. He sat and listened to the local Muslim leaders, proclaiming the strength of Islam over Christianity. Which will survive, speakers asked—Islam, standing for freedom, justice, and equality, or

Christianity, standing for slavery, suffering, and death? The answer was clear. Yet too few blacks were hearing the message. There were too many empty seats. Malcolm wanted to pull in every black in Detroit. If each could hear Allah's ideas and teachings, it would end the drinking, fighting, and drug use that had destroyed so many lives.

Malcolm's official application for Muslim membership sailed through swiftly. From the Chicago home office, he received his "X"—a symbol of the true African name he had never known. Little had been a slave owner's name, given to all the slaves of a white slave owner long ago. Now Malcolm was a Muslim, and in the nation of Islam, he would be known as Malcolm X. Someday God would provide him with a holy name from His own mouth.

One morning Malcolm rose early. A caravan of Detroit cars filled with Muslims was heading to Chicago. Elijah Muhammad was scheduled to speak. Malcolm could hardly contain himself.

Temple Two was filled with hundreds of worshipers. Excitement was in the air. Malcolm's eyes widened as he watched Elijah Muhammad approach the platform. The man was small, in his mid-60s, dressed in a white shirt, bow tie, and dark suit. On his head he wore a gold-embroidered fez.

As Elijah Muhammad spoke, Malcolm leaned

forward in his chair, eager to take in every word. The
Muslim leader spoke of his own time in prison, jailed
for speaking the truth, condemned in a white man's
world. He told of how the white man had held all
blacks back, stripping them of their heritage and
culture, casting away their identity. Then he singled
out Malcolm himself. He testified to Malcolm's
devotion and how he had written daily while he was in
prison. Mr. Muhammad publicly declared his belief
that Malcolm would remain faithful.

Once back in Detroit, Malcolm felt a new calling.
He wanted to build up the Muslim membership, to
bring every black to Allah. Even those blacks not
actively involved with the Muslim faith knew of it.
Malcolm took it as his own personal cause to take Allah
and the Islam faith to all of his fellow blacks. It might
take time and energy, but Malcolm did not care. It was
his calling, his mission.

Malcolm's work on behalf of Elijah Muhammad
captured every moment of his thinking time. After
leaving the furniture store, Malcolm worked for Ford
Motor Company. But as far as money was concerned,
all he wanted was enough to stay alive and pay his bills.
The white man owned most of the business world in
America, and by this time Malcolm had no use for the
white man at all.

It was Elijah Muhammad Malcolm wanted to

work for, and early in the 1950s, the eager young follower got his chance. He was invited to Chicago to train as a Muslim minister.

Malcolm could not have wished for more. During the months he studied in Chicago, he came to know all the important aspects of the Muslim faith—the need for purity and sacrifice in daily life; that is, to have a clean soul and spirit one must have a clean mind and body. Prayer would always provide support for such a goal, for Allah hears all and knows all. Malcolm came to understand the roles of men and women, the uses of the Bible and the Koran. He learned how Muslims could be organized, new temples formed, and the faith spread among others.

To the foundations of the Muslim faith itself, Malcolm applied his own creed. It was not enough merely to preach and teach about Allah; it was necessary to destroy the hold of the white man on blacks. Again Malcolm turned to the history of black slavery in America, the degradation of blacks at the white man's hands, and the revenge that was needed to make things even. He practiced his own style of preaching when he was sent to Muslim meetings on the East Coast.

With force and energy, Malcolm spoke out against the hold the white man kept over the black man. "The white man is the devil, always has been, always will be,"

Malcolm raged. "Watch him. Do not let him exploit us as he has been doing. He is evil."

Elijah Muhammad saw in Malcolm a powerful force for the cause of the Muslim faith. Sent to Boston to organize the blacks there, Malcolm did not waste a moment. From meeting time to meeting time, the numbers of the attendees increased. Malcolm smiled broadly when he heard chairs were rented because of the growing crowds.

From Boston it was to Philadelphia, then back to Detroit, and a stay in Chicago. More and more local Muslim officials asked for Malcolm X. Whenever he spoke, big crowds came to listen.

Malcolm was glad to hear such reports. Yet he knew it was essential to stay focused on the faith and his mission. Elijah Muhammad often warned against envy and jealousy among those around him. Malcolm made it a point to mention Allah by name at least once a minute when he spoke.

Nonetheless, Malcolm's face began to appear in newspapers and magazines across the country. He was labeled "The New Black Voice" by some editors and reporters. Followers of the civil rights leader Martin Luther King, Jr., cautioned Malcolm about stirring up hatred by his outspoken criticism of whites. But Malcolm refused to tone down his speeches. He spoke out against integration, insisting that most blacks did not want to live side by side with the white man. Instead, Malcolm declared, the majority of blacks wanted human rights and respect as human beings. That's what America's black masses wanted in day-to-day living. He criticized the way Martin Luther King, Jr., and others seemed willing to "cozy up" to white leaders.

In June of 1954, Malcolm received word he was going to head up Temple Seven in New York City. It was a big responsibility. New York's boroughs contained over a million black people. What a potential for gathering followers for Allah! But there was much work ahead. Few black people had ever heard of the Islamic faith and Muslims.

Malcolm did not waste a moment. He organized his strongest followers in the area, scheduled meetings, had pamphlets printed, then went out to speak to other groups or anyone on the street who would listen. With everything he did, there was a force and determination. Yet it was clear that this was much more than a campaign for Allah; it was a campaign against the white man. Within the inner circles of leadership surrounding Elijah Muhammad, there were whispers about Malcolm. Some people close to Elijah Muhammad suggested Malcolm wanted power and publicity for himself.

Malcolm heard the rumors, and he tried to ignore them. Elijah Muhammad had told him there would be those who would envy him. Sure enough, that was true. But Malcolm was determined not to let that get in his way.

There were other thoughts in Malcolm's mind. Ever since he had been released from prison, there had been little time for women in his life. Yet it was now impossible to ignore a recent addition to the Temple Seven membership. Sister Betty X was a native of Detroit, more recently a student at Alabama's Tuskegee Institute. She had come to New York City to study nursing. Whenever she could, she presented talks to the Muslim women about medicine and hygiene.

At first Malcolm spoke only briefly to Sister Betty X, discussing her work with the temple members. But it was soon clear enough that he cared for her deeply. Although she did not quite measure up to what Elijah Muhammad thought a suitable couple should be (a wife's ideal age should be half the man's age plus seven, for example), Malcolm shared his feelings about Betty X with the Muslim leader. Elijah Muhammad asked to meet this sister. When he did, he gave his approval. On January 15, 1958, Malcolm X and Betty X were married in Michigan.

There was little time for a honeymoon. Malcolm was soon back at work, speaking and giving directions to those at Temple Seven in New York City. Although those around him seemed pleased with the steady growth in attendance, Malcolm was not. He was always impatient, looking for ways to speed up everything.

In November of 1958, Malcolm and Betty welcomed their first child. They named her Attilah, after the famed chieftain who waged attacks on Rome centuries ago. Shortly afterward, they found a seven-room house in Queens, a borough of New York City.

There were never enough hours in the day for Malcolm. Newspaper and magazine reporters wanted interviews, and radio and television people did, too. Malcolm gave as many as possible. He always insisted that the spotlight be directed on Elijah Muhammad and the nation of Islam.

Despite his attempts to diminish his own role, Malcolm often found himself in the forefront of whatever article appeared. He was news, there was no doubt about it. His angry outbursts against whites, his attacks against Christianity—these were what captured the headlines. The tongues at Elijah Muhammad's headquarters continued to wag, criticizing Malcolm for promoting himself. In 1959, television viewers found themselves watching a program entitled "The Hate That Hate Produced." Elijah Muhammad, Malcolm, the Muslims—all were portrayed as part of some sinister force, alive and growing in America, a cause for fear and concern. Newspapers and magazines followed up the program with blazing headlines and articles full of half-truths, always sensationalizing the black Muslims.

Indeed, it was always black Muslims who were portrayed as being racists, superracists, anti-Christians, white haters. The American public stirred with unrest.

Again and again, Malcolm was hit with reporters' queries: "Why do you teach black supremacy?" "Why do you promote hate?" The questions angered Malcolm. Why were *his* beliefs and feelings so important? Couldn't the white man recognize his own ugly past, his inexcusable treatment of blacks in America? Where was the confusion? It was so clear, so perfectly clear. Those same reporters then seemed to push their stories aside and become defense attorneys for the white race, trying to defend themselves and their own past.

Malcolm's anger poured over, anger against the media for constantly portraying the nation of Islam in America, the Muslim cause, in such a sinister light. He grew equally annoyed with the quiet calm and patience of Elijah Muhammad, always softly answering questions and accusations, forever promoting Allah, the faith, the dreams and goals. Did Elijah never tire of the white man's ways, Malcolm wondered, and want to fire back? It never seemed so.

Malcolm continued to scoff at talk of "integration." It was such a hoax, such a lie. He insisted that blacks wanted no part of integration, that it was impossible to achieve and was not a desirable end anyway. Malcolm argued that blacks would be better off with "complete separation."

"Complete separation." After all that had been accomplished? What about the noted 1954 Supreme Court decision about school segregation? Surely that was a major advancement for the black people. Martin Luther King, Jr., had said so, and so had other leaders, black and white. To Malcolm, integration was nothing but a fraud. It looked good and sounded good, but it was a joke. It was just another law filled with loopholes that would never benefit black people.

Early in 1963, Malcolm was asked to write his life story with the help of noted black author Alex Haley. Malcolm gave the matter careful thought. Finally he agreed, as long as Mr. Muhammad thought it was all right and as long as the nation of Islam received all profits Malcolm might receive from the book. Mr. Muhammad agreed, expressing his appreciation to his devoted minister.

Those close to Elijah Muhammad had become very concerned about his health. Often he shook with coughing spells, and weight slipped from his already frail body. Malcolm and other Muslim leaders could not hide their concern. The thought of the nation of Islam in America without Elijah Muhammad could hardly be imagined. He was, in Malcolm's view, black America's moral, mental, and spiritual reformer.

But in July of 1963, the media revealed the facts of a legal case that shocked Malcolm X. Two secretaries in the Muslim movement charged that Elijah Muhammad had fathered their four children. For six years, he had supposedly been conducting affairs that completely contradicted the Muslim concepts of morality. Malcolm could not believe the charges. Could this be the same person who had expelled his brother Reginald for immoral actions so many years ago?

Naturally the media thrust the news of Elijah Muhammad into the world spotlight. The reaction was swift and immediate. Muslims quickly began to drop from the membership rolls. Concerned as he was, Malcolm sought interviews with the secretaries who had brought the charges against Elijah Muhammad. Malcolm wanted to hear for himself from the women. Despite the fact that they were officially "in isolation" within the faith, Malcolm broke the rules. Learning of this, Elijah Muhammad was angry.

Before this outburst had subsided, America suffered another tragic blow. In November, an assassin cut down the president of the United States, John F. Kennedy, while he rode in a motorcade in Dallas. Media people sought out all political and spiritual leaders for comment. Elijah Muhammad advised his Muslim officials to keep quiet about the entire event. But Malcolm could not be silenced. How many times had he been accused of stirring up hatred, of pitting blacks against whites, Muslims against Christians?

Again and again, his words had been played with,
rearranged, taken out of context. Now he spoke loudly.
"The chickens have come home to roost," he told
reporters about Kennedy's death, meaning such a
happening was inevitable. Malcolm blasted away at
the white man's hate. According to Malcolm, the hate
of the white man had often destroyed the black
man and held him back. Now, that same hate had
killed the president.

It was not what a country in turmoil needed to
hear. People were outraged. So was Elijah Muhammad,
who was still angry about Malcolm's personal
investigation into the Muslim leader's activities. He
summoned Malcolm to his headquarters and imposed
a 90-day period of silence on him. He had to refrain
from all public pronouncements and activities.

Elijah Muhammad's actions stunned Malcolm.
He felt he had been so true, so faithful. Now he was
being disciplined for speaking his mind, sharing his
thoughts. He felt angry and betrayed. All the years of
devotion seemed to be tossed away, unappreciated.
Finally Malcolm made a decision. He would split with
Elijah Muhammad. But his work for Allah would continue.

Malcolm summoned reporters to a press
conference. He announced plans to open a new mosque
in New York City. Within this center of worship, a
fresh base would be established for all devoted Muslims.

Where would the new mosque be located? For the time being, Muslim Mosque, Inc., would be set up in the Hotel Theresa in Harlem. From that spot Malcolm X hoped actively to attack all those forces holding back 22 million African Americans.

It was done. The break with Elijah Muhammad was complete. It was not only a sad parting, but one that Malcolm recognized would be dangerous. Always, there had been those who hated him for his campaign against white supremacy and his outbursts against Christian attitudes. Now Malcolm knew there were those within the Muslim community who would feel he was a traitor. But Malcolm felt he had done what was necessary.

Still another mission was necessary. Every Muslim hopes someday to make a pilgrimage, or Haji to Mecca, the holy city. Malcolm felt drawn to make such a journey. Malcolm had fathered three daughters, and money for such a trip was not easily available. Once again his sister Ella volunteered to help with expenses.

The trip was the most moving experience of his life. Joining pilgrims of all sizes and shapes, of all races and colors, Malcolm was just one more brother going to bear witness to the beloved Allah. He flew first to Frankfurt, Germany, then on to Cairo, where he went sight-seeing for two days. Yet he could not keep his thoughts off the real purpose of his journey. From Cairo, the plane flew to Jeddah, a town on the

Red Sea in Saudi Arabia. Mecca lay inland, some 40 miles to the east.

Finally, Malcolm arrived. As an American Muslim, he sensed a special respect given him. Others observed him closely, inspecting his every move, wanting him to be comfortable. But Malcolm cast away that awareness of the outside world. He had come to pray, to commune with Allah. Other thoughts were left behind.

The days that followed found Malcolm in constant reflection. Most pilgrims prayed in Arabic, a language Malcolm knew only slightly. He mumbled the words as best he could, but he did not care. His heart and soul were speaking, not his voice. He clothed himself in the Mecca pilgrim's attire, the ihram, which consists of two towels and sandals. Never had Malcolm seen such sincere and true brotherhood among people of all races. The white man did not seem the source of evil he had seemed in the past. Standing on Mount Arafat brought a true feeling of joy, the climax of the pilgrim's trip to Mecca. There was no color difference, no awareness of the past. Malcolm was totally immersed in a feeling of love. He felt cleansed, and the hatred of the white man seemed to disappear. Before he left, Prince Faisal of Arabia invited him for a personal audience. Once again, Malcolm knew he was not just an ordinary American, a typical Muslim. He was special.

Then the trip was over. Yet pilgrim friends he had

made insisted that he join them on still another journey in the spring of 1964. He flew to Africa this time, to Nigeria, and Ghana, homeland of his ancestors. He felt a closeness there, too, a link with the past. His hosts welcomed him warmly and hated to bid him farewell.

But there was work to be done at home. He approached the weeks of 1965 with new vigor, and although he knew there was much mending to be done to rebuild the torn Muslim fences, he felt ready. There were speeches to be given, more interviews to share. Maybe, just maybe, people would listen.

But there was something in the air. Malcolm sensed that time was running out. He wanted to finish his story, his autobiography, so that people would know and understand. If only there was time, he thought.

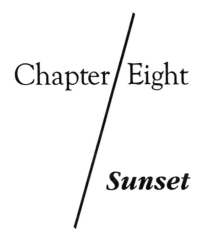

Chapter / Eight

Sunset

Meetings, speeches, words, people—for Malcolm X, each day flowed smoothly into another. But it was not as easy now. Donations were not flowing in as he'd hoped for the work to be done. Sometimes contributions did not even pay for the hall that was rented for a Muslim gathering. Empty chairs. How he remembered those empty chairs from the days back in Detroit. Well, they would be filled again. Malcolm was determined to see that happen.

It was that determination that brought him to Harlem's Audubon Ballroom on February 21, 1965. Again, the audience was smaller than he had hoped, but when he took to the podium, the numbers vanished. He could talk to 200 as easily as he could talk to 2,000.

But on this particular Sunday afternoon, Malcolm

X spoke to no one. Bullets ripped through his body before he got the chance. That evening, while people watched their television sets, the announcement came.

"Black nationalist and Muslim leader Malcolm X was gunned down this afternoon in New York's Harlem. News of his death has just been confirmed by officials of Columbia University Hospital who . . . "

Many failed to hear the details. The surprise of Malcolm X's death was too shocking. In Chicago, Elijah Muhammad was contacted for a statement about his former minister. "No comment," came the curt reply.

Two days later, thousands of mourners passed by the body of Malcolm X, otherwise known as El-Haji Malik El-Shabazz, also known as Malcolm Little, at the Unity Funeral Home in Harlem. His wife, Betty, pregnant with a fourth child and trying to comfort her three daughters, was a poignant sight. "She's a black Jacqueline Kennedy," one observer remarked, recalling the courage shown by the late president's widow two years earlier.

The funeral was held at the Faith Temple, Church of God in Christ, a former movie theater. Afterward the body was transported to the Ferncliff Cemetery in Ardsley, New York. Christian mourners stood in silent prayer at the grave site, while the Muslims knelt with their foreheads pressed to the ground in the Eastern tradition of worship.

In the weeks that followed, the assassins of Malcolm X were apprehended. Talmadge Hayer, Norman Butler, and Thomas Johnson were accused of being active black Muslims out to silence a black Muslim competitor. In 1966, they were brought to trial and found guilty of murder in the first degree.

But somehow, people didn't seem to care about those who had brought about the death of Malcolm X. He was gone, that was the fact of the matter. Gone was the man who called himself "the angriest man in America." He was no longer angry. The black rage was over.

Now he was at peace.

Selected Bibliography

Alexander, Rae Pace, ed. *Young and Black in America.* New York: Random House, 1970.

Breitman, George. *The Last Year of Malcolm X: The Evolution of a Revolutionary.* New York: Pathfinder Press, 1970.

Goldman, Peter. *The Death and Life of Malcolm X.* Champaign, Ill.: University of Illinois Press, 1979.

Rummel, Jack. *Malcolm X.* Black Americans of Achievement Series. Philadelphia: Chelsea House, 1989.

White, Florence M. *Malcolm X: Black and Proud.* Americans All Series. Champaign, Ill.: Garrard Publishing, 1965.

X, Malcolm. *The Autobiography of Malcolm X.* New York: Grove Press, 1965.

Index